WITHDRAWN

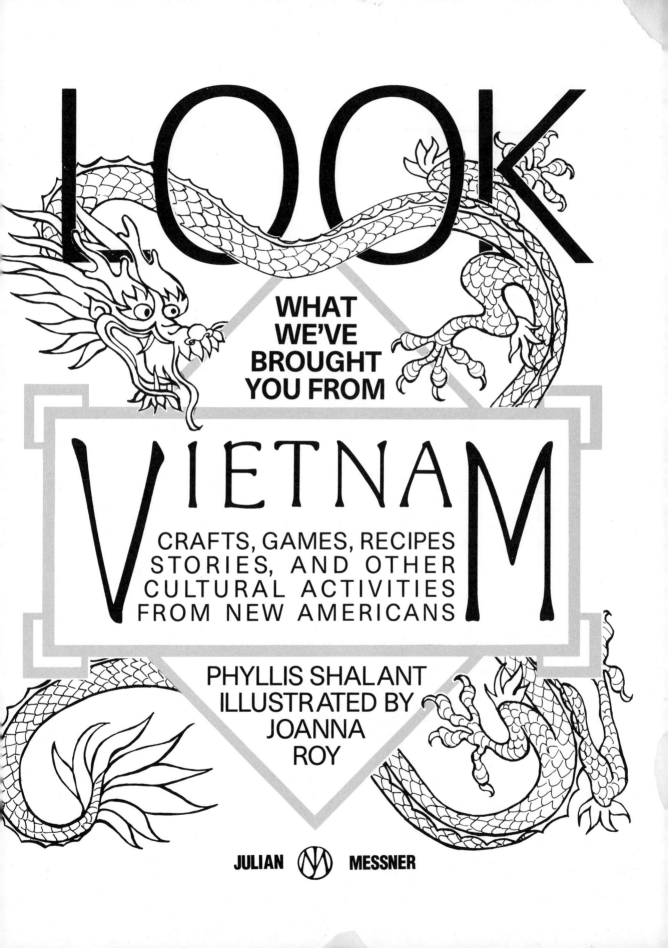

LOOK

WHAT WE'VE BROUGHT YOU FROM

VIETNAM

CRAFTS, GAMES, RECIPES
STORIES, AND OTHER
CULTURAL ACTIVITIES
FROM NEW AMERICANS

PHYLLIS SHALANT
ILLUSTRATED BY
JOANNA
ROY

JULIAN Ⓜ MESSNER

Copyright © 1988 by Phyllis Shalant. All rights
reserved including the right of reproduction in
whole or in part in any form. Published by Julian
Messner, a Division of Simon & Schuster,
Simon & Schuster Building, Rockefeller Center,
1230 Avenue of the Americas, New York,
NY 10020. JULIAN MESSNER and colophon are
trademarks of Simon & Schuster.

Designed by Malle N. Whitaker.

Manufactured in the United States of America.

10 9 8 7 6 5 4 3 2 1—Lib. ed.
10 9 8 7 6 5 4 3   —Paper ed.

Library of Congress Cataloging in Publication Data
Shalant, Phyllis.
Look what we've brought you from Vietnam.
Includes index.
Summary: Introduces Vietnam's cultural
background with games, folk tales, recipes,
puppets, and crafts.
    1. Creative activities and seat work—Vietnam—
Juvenile literature. [1. Handicraft—Vietnam.
2. Cookery, Vietnamese. 3. Folklore—Vietnam.
4. Games. 5. Vietnam—Social life and customs]
I. Title.
GV1204.73.S52   1988   372.8'3   87-20276
ISBN 0-671-63919-6 Lib. ed.
        0-671-65978-2 Paper ed.

ACKNOWLEDGMENTS

The information in this book comes both from private individuals and public sources. Special thanks are due to Nganh Huynh, who arrived here from Vietnam in 1979 and is now a college student. In addition, I received a wealth of help and information from Melinda Greenblatt and Janet Smith at the Information Center on Children's Cultures of the United States Committee for UNICEF. Laurie Kuntz, a teacher of English at a refugee camp in Manila and an author of some very successful ESL material, was also generous with her assistance. Thanks are also due to my husband, Herbert Shalant, for technical advice in adapting many of the crafts activities.

CONTENTS

INTRODUCTION

Between 1976 and 1990, 471,850 Vietnamese immigrants came to settle in the United States. Today they live in every one of the fifty states. Perhaps they are your neighbors, or even your classmates.

Why did they leave Vietnam? They fled from a long, terrible war between the governments of the north and the south for control of the country. The war endangered their lives and destroyed their villages, homes, and possessions.

These new Americans may have left many things behind when they said good-bye to their native country, but they all brought along something very important—their culture. This book includes things to make and do from the culture of Vietnam. Although many of the activities may seem unusual at first—who knows, maybe someday soon you'll invite your friends over to play O-Lang (page 22) with you!

THE SHAPE OF VIETNAM

The outline of Vietnam on a map is often compared to a *don ganh*, a long pole with a rice basket hanging at each end that farmers carry over their shoulder. The fertile deltas of the Red River in the northern end of the country and the Mekong River in the southwest are Vietnam's rice baskets. The long, skinny stretch of land connecting these deltas is the "pole." Vietnam covers 128,000 square miles and is about the size of the state of New Mexico.

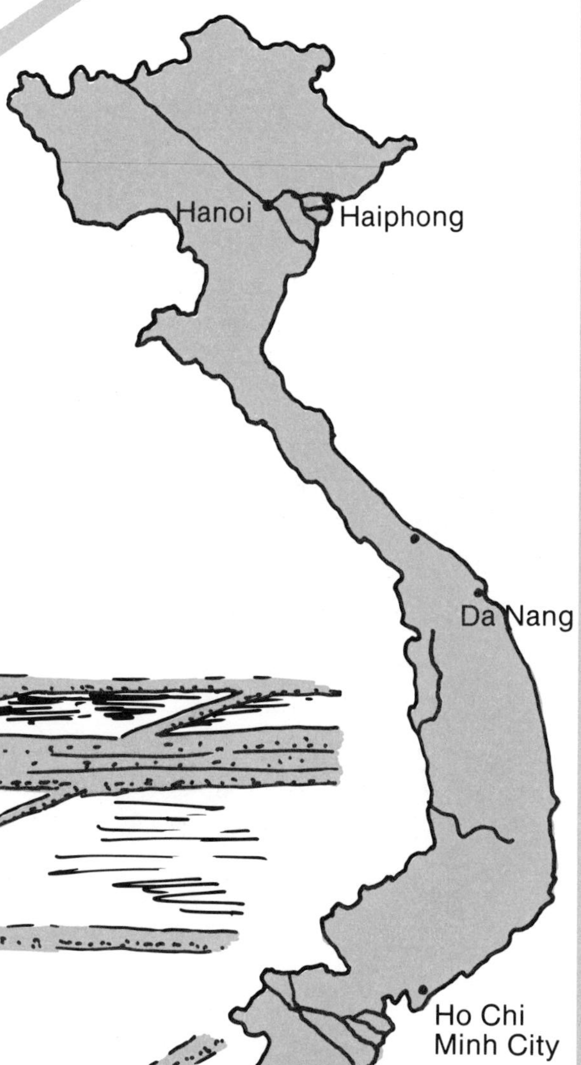

Hanoi

Haiphong

Da Nang

Ho Chi Minh City

HOLIDAY FUN

TET NGUYEN-DEN—THE NEW YEAR

Many Vietnamese customs actually come from China, which long ago ruled Vietnam for 1,000 years. The people of Vietnam use the Chinese calendar system, based on the moon. The New Year, Tet Nguyen-Den (usually just called Tet) falls between January 20 and February 20. It starts at the second new moon after the beginning of winter.

Tet is the most important holiday in Vietnam and is celebrated for at least three days. Houses are cleaned from top to bottom. Everyone shops and spends money lavishly on food, new clothing, and gifts. Delicious banquets are cooked and served, including the traditional square rice cakes known as *banh chung.* Children receive gifts of money in bright red envelopes.

The night before the New Year everyone stays up very late. At the stroke of midnight they must be doing something good, because their deeds at that moment represent their fortune for the year to come. The Vietnamese believe that the protective spirits of their household—much like guardian angels— rise up to heaven to report on the good and bad deeds of each member of the family.

On New Year's Day, the first visitor to each house is very important. The Vietnamese hope that person will bring them good luck for the coming year. If a wealthy visitor is first to enter your home, perhaps his good fortune will rub off on you! On the third day of Tet, each family lights long, thin incense sticks that burn slowly, giving off a fragrant farewell to the spirits of their ancestors who came to earth for a New Year's visit. For children, the highlight of Tet is the dragon dance—a sort of parade that comes down the street at night. The dragon, a good luck symbol, wears a costume made of a papier-mâché head and a brightly colored silk train. The dancers under the costume must be very agile, because during their dance they perform acrobatic feats. They climb up high poles to reach traditional bundles of flags, vegetables, and money that the villagers have hung for them.

Make a Dragon Puppet for Tet

MATERIALS:

Red or other colored construction paper rectangle, 5½″ x 8½″
5 strips of colored ribbon, 1½″ wide; one 4 feet long, four 2 feet long

Construction or origami paper for eyes, tongue, and teeth
Glue
Plastic drinking straw

INSTRUCTIONS:

HEAD

1. Hold rectangle lengthwise and fold in half.
2. Fold upper left and right corners down, leaving about a ½″ border at bottom.
3. Open figure at bottom. Fold front border up over folded corners. Now turn figure over and fold up back border.
4. Turn figure on its side. Open and fold in half vertically.
5. Using paper of a different color, cut out eyes, pointed teeth, and long, arrow-shaped tongue and glue onto head.

1.

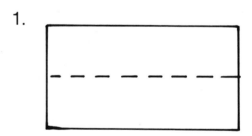

2.

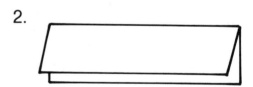

3.

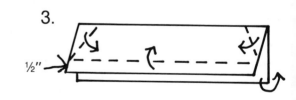

½″ →

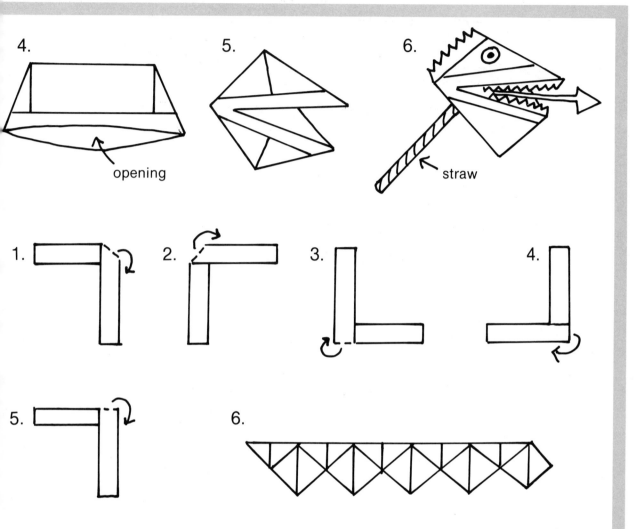

4.

opening

5.

6.

straw

1.

2.

3.

4.

5.

6.

BODY AND LEGS

1. Find middle of 4-foot ribbon. Fold right side over and down to form diagonal corner.
2. Turn over to back side.
3. Fold up strip now hanging down.
4. Fold horizontal strip over toward left.
5. Fold vertical strip down over horizontal. Continue until ribbon is folded into a single square.

6. Hold both ends and pull apart. This is the body. Attach to back of head.
7. Fold ribbon legs in same manner. Attach to body.
8. Cut out four paper claw feet and attach to legs.
9. Poke hole in underside of head. Insert straw. Your dragon is ready to march!

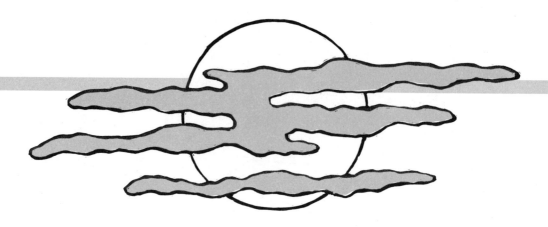

TET TRUNG-THU—
THE MID-AUTUMN FESTIVAL

In late September or early October, when the moon is at its brightest, the people of Vietnam celebrate Tet Trung-Thu. In the Chinese lunar calendar, this holiday falls on the fifteenth day of the eighth month. Tet Trung-Thu is a favorite of the children of Vietnam. To honor the moon, traditional "moon cakes" are eaten and given as gifts. On page 28, you'll find a recipe for making this delicious treat. At Tet Trung-Thu, children spend their time creating lanterns shaped like boats, cranes, dragons, hares, unicorns, carp—every imaginable creature or object. At night, lighted candles are placed inside these lanterns and the children march through the streets with them to the rhythms of drums and cymbals.

A LANTERN FOR TET TRUNG-THU

You can light this simple boat lantern with a flashlight instead of a candle.

MATERIALS:

Square of colored construction paper or origami paper, 6″ or larger
Rectangle of oaktag or other heavy paper, 8½″ x 11″

Masking tape
Stapler
Flashlight

INSTRUCTIONS:

BOAT
1. Fold square in half to create center line.
2. Reopen. Now fold each half of square toward center to create a rectangle. Be careful not to overlap folds.
3. Fold each corner down toward center opening.
4. Fold new corners that have been created toward center again.
5. Fold triangle tips down toward center.
6. To finish, carefully turn your boat inside out.

LANTERN
1. Roll oaktag into cylinder. Tape or staple closed.
2. Stand cylinder up and tape or staple boat to top of cylinder.
3. Point flashlight up into bottom of cylinder and attach using masking tape.

You are now ready to join the Tet Trung-Thu parade!

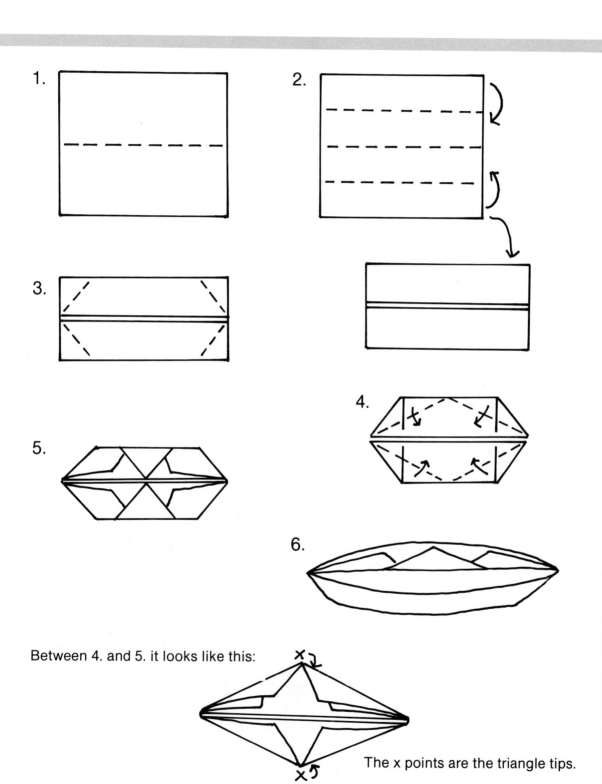

1.

2.

3.

4.

5.

6.

Between 4. and 5. it looks like this:

The x points are the triangle tips.

MORE FUN VIETNAMESE STYLE

FLY A KITCHEN KITE

Kite flying is popular all over Asia. The kites range from very beautiful and complicated, to very simple and homey. Here is an easy-to-make Vietnamese kite made of kitchen materials. One Vietnamese girl says she made one "whenever I could snatch my mother's incense sticks." Ask an adult to help you find supplies you need. You can substitute bamboo for incense sticks. The wax paper, which is very light, makes this kite a good flier.

MATERIALS:

Roll of wax paper, 12″ wide
Two bamboo sticks, each about 24″ long
(available at most florist shops)
Ball of string, kite twine or fishing line
Cotton cloth for making tail (old sheet or
pillowcase works well)
White glue
Stapler

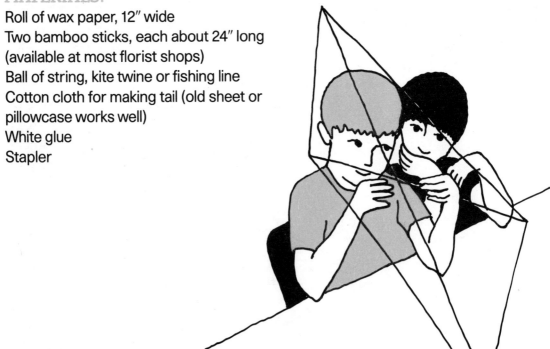

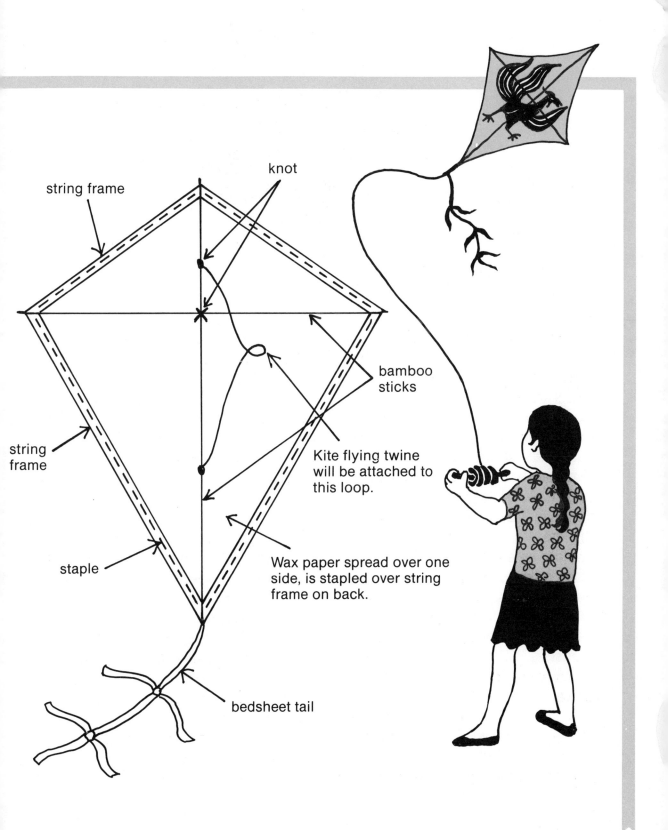

knot

string frame

string frame

staple

bamboo sticks

Kite flying twine will be attached to this loop.

Wax paper spread over one side, is stapled over string frame on back.

bedsheet tail

17

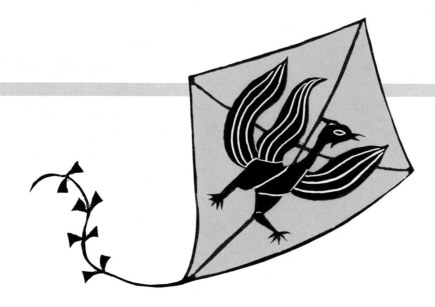

INSTRUCTIONS:

1. Shorten one of the bamboo sticks to about three quarters of the length of the other stick. For example, if your sticks are 24″ long, shorten one to 18″. Now make a mark at 18″, or three quarters of the way up the longer stick, and lay the shorter stick across it at that point to make a cross. Use string to tie the crossed bamboo sticks firmly together. This makes the frame of the kite.

2. Have an adult make a slit with a razor blade or knife about ¼″ deep on all four ends of the frame. Unroll enough string to run around frame, making a diamond shape. Wedge string into each of the four slits. Pull string taut around frame.

3. Roll out and tear off two long sheets of wax paper (each about 26″ long if you have used 24″ bamboo sticks). Lay the sheets out side by side, overlapping one about 1½″ over the other. Glue the sheets together, making sure to seal the seams on both sides.

4. When the glue is dry, lay the bamboo frame down on top of the paper. Fold paper into diamond shape to cover one side of the frame, keeping bamboo tips exposed. Paper edges should just cover string. Crease paper, staple or glue down along crease.

5. Cut a string approximately 12″ long and knot a small loop in the center. Now tie one end to longer stick about 1″ above point where sticks cross. Tie the other end to the center point between opposite end of stick and place where sticks cross. The kite-flying twine will be attached to the small loop at the center of this string.

6. Make a tail about 24″ long from a strip of the cotton cloth. Tie to bottom of center stick. Attach your kite-flying twine to small loop.

Now try out your kite on the first breezy day!

19

CATCH A CRICKET

June in Vietnam is a time for crickets. Vietnamese children scour the fields looking for male crickets to use in competitions or matches. At a cricket match, two male crickets are placed in the same cage and encouraged to fight, but if you're lucky enough to find one, you can just keep this harmless singing creature as a summer pet.

Begin your search for a cricket when the weather gets warm. Two of the most commonly found crickets in the United States are the house cricket, a yellowish-gray and brown creature about one inch long, found living under stones, logs, porches and in people's houses; and the field cricket, black headed with a black or blackish-brown body and bronze-colored wings, found in gardens and fields. You can house your cricket in an old aquarium or deep glass jar. The floor of the jar should be covered with about an inch of soil and a few small stones and dry leaves. Cover the top of the jar with plastic wrap in which some holes have been punched for air. Be sure to place just one cricket in your cricket house, because if you happen to place two of the same sex in a single container, they may fight to the death.

Crickets eat an amazing variety of things! Fresh or even decaying vegetables like lettuce and cucumbers, soft fruits like bananas, soft cheese and bread crumbs can all be offered (in portions no bigger than a nickel), and a bottle cap filled with water makes a good drinking dish. When the weather begins to turn cold, bring your cricket indoors to keep it healthy.

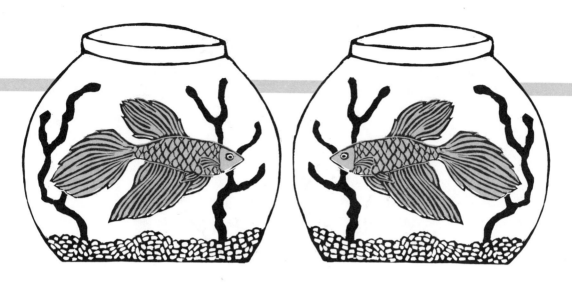

FIGHTING FISH

Fighting fish are common in Vietnam. You can find these beautiful creatures in American pet shops, too, but they are much more expensive here. Vietnamese children sometimes hold matches between these fighting pets. Each fighting fish is kept separately in its own very small bowl, about the size of a grapefruit. To hold a "fight," two fish bowls are placed side by side with a sheet of paper between them so that the fish cannot see each other. At the signal, the paper is removed. Although the fish cannot touch each other, they "fight" by displaying their long beautiful fins and thrashing about in their bowls. The winning fish is the one that does not back down.

O-LANG—COUNT AND CAPTURE

In Vietnam the gameboard for O-lang may be twelve small holes dug in the ground, and the playing pieces (called counters here) may be seeds, pebbles, or shells. But for holes, you can use paper cups, and for counters you can use sunflower or pumpkin seeds, peanuts or breakfast cereal. That way you can eat your winnings.

MATERIALS:

Twelve paper cups
70 sunflower seeds or other small counters

TO SET UP:

Each player lines up a row of six paper cups. The rows should be side by side. The cup at the top of each line is called the mansion. Put 10 counters in each mansion. Then put five counters in each of the other cups. You are ready to begin.

TO PLAY:

1. First player begins at any cup in either row, excluding the mansion. He takes all five counters from this cup and, moving clockwise, drops one in each of the next cups in both rows until his hand is empty. Now he takes the counters from the next cup ahead and repeats this *until the last counter dropped is followed by an empty cup.*

2. When the last counter dropped is followed by an empty cup, the player skips that cup and picks up all the counters in the next cup. These are his winnings. If his "winnings" cup is followed by another empty-full pair,

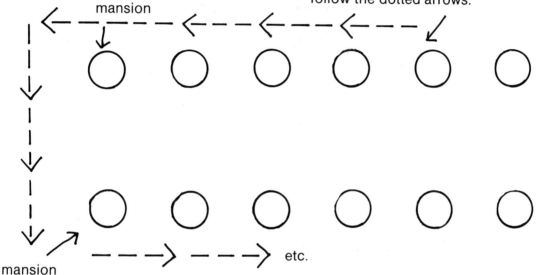

If player decides to start here, the counter-clockwise progression would follow the dotted arrows.

mansion

mansion

etc.

or a series of them, he captures the counters in those cups, too. Now his turn is over. He should put his winnings aside.

3. The next player begins his turn, starting wherever he chooses, repeating the same procedure as player number one.

4. The game ends when one player has lost all the counters in his cups and his mansion. Both players should then count their winnings. The one with the most pieces is the winner.

SPECIAL RULES TO REMEMBER:

♦ The mansion may not be used to start a game.

♦ If a player's last counter is dropped in the empty cup before a mansion, his turn ends with no winnings. The mansion can only be captured if the cup before it is empty and the last counter in the player's hand falls into the second cup before the mansion.

♦ If a player runs out of counters in his cups *but still has counters in his mansion*, he may borrow counters from his winnings.

BITE THE CARP'S TAIL

The carp is a popular fish all over Asia. It is a symbol of good luck, often kept as a pet. The Vietnamese version of this playground or gym game needs at least six players, but it's possible for an entire class to play. The longer the line, the more fun you'll have.

TO PLAY:

1. Have players form a single line, one behind the other with hands on each other's hips. The first person is the carp's head, the last person is the carp's tail.

2. When everyone is ready, the head must try to "bite" the tail by catching hold of it. To avoid capture, the end of the line will swing and coil away from the head, but the line may not break; each player must hold tight to the person in front of him or her at all times.

3. When the tail is bitten (caught), the head goes to the back of the line to become the new tail and the player who was second in line is the new head.

LET'S EAT

♦ BE SURE A RESPONSIBLE ADULT HAS GIVEN YOU PERMISSION TO USE THE STOVE OR HOT PLATE.

Nuoc mam, a brown sauce made from fermented fish, is the trademark of Vietnamese cooking. It is the main ingredient in *nuoc cham,* a dressing and table sauce that the Vietnamese eat with all foods, probably more often than you use ketchup! Rice and fish are basic foods in Vietnam. The Vietnamese also like to serve many uncooked vegetables in salads or pickled. Many fresh herbs and spices, including basil, mint, coriander, ginger, chili peppers, and garlic give Vietnamese food its distinctive flavor and add color to many dishes. Lemon grass, which looks like scallions, gives Vietnamese food a lemony tang.

Try to visit a Vietnamese restaurant if there is one in your area. Or you can try Vietnamese food at home by preparing these two favorites.

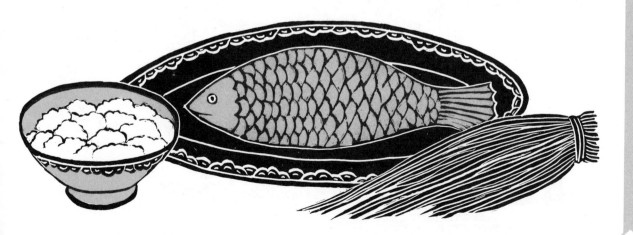

CHAO—CHICKEN AND LONG RICE SOUP

INGREDIENTS:

1 large cooked chicken breast
½ lb. long rice (often called cellophane noodles—you can find them in Oriental food stores *or* you can substitute Italian vermicelli noodles)

2 scallions
5 cups chicken broth
1 tablespoon soy sauce
½ tsp. salt; ⅛ tsp. pepper

UTENSILS:

Knife
Large serving bowl
Medium saucepan
Measuring cups
Measuring spoons
Mixing spoon

DIRECTIONS:

1. Remove skin from cooked chicken breast and slice meat into thin strips.
2. If using long rice, soak in warm water for 10 minutes. Drain and break into pieces. If using vermicelli, cook until tender following directions on package.
3. Put noodles in bowl.
4. Rinse whole scallions and chop into small bits.

5. Pour chicken broth into saucepan and bring to boil. Stir in soy sauce. Season with salt and pepper. Add the cooked chicken strips and chopped scallions. Cook all together for one minute over medium heat.
6. Pour the soup over the noodles. Enjoy!

MOON CAKES

Traditional moon cakes are treats eaten to honor the moon during Tet Trung-Thu. There are two basic kinds of moon cakes in Vietnam, baked and unbaked, but every family has their own favorite fillings to put inside. Here is a very simple recipe for one version of the unbaked kind. You can decide what filling to put in the center—diced bananas, peanuts, raisins, sugar, or if you can find them, candied lotus seeds.

INGREDIENTS:

2 cups glutinous rice (also called sweet rice—you can get this in an Oriental grocery store)
3/4 cup coconut cream
1 teaspoon sugar
1/2 teaspoon salt
Fillings (see above)

UTENSILS:

Measuring cup
Measuring spoons
2-quart saucepan
Mixing spoon
Aluminum foil
Steamer
Teaspoon

DIRECTIONS:

1. Put rice in 2-quart saucepan, cover with hot tap water, and soak for one hour. Then drain well.

2. Mix coconut cream, sugar, and salt into rice. Cook over medium heat for about 10 minutes, stirring frequently. The rice should be only half cooked. Remove from heat and let cool.

3. When rice is *completely* cool, take a handful and shape into a ball. Make a hole or pocket in the center with your thumb. Put in about 1/2 tsp. of filling of your choice. Then press rice together so that filling is hidden in the middle of the ball. Repeat with remaining rice and filling.

4. Wrap each rice ball in aluminum foil. Place in a steamer.

5. HAVE AN ADULT HELP YOU WITH THIS PART. Steam over boiling water for 40 minutes or until the rice is soft. Your mooncakes are now ready. Be careful when opening foil because very hot steam will escape.

A VIETNAMESE FOLKTALE

WHY THE MONSOON COMES EVERY YEAR

Throughout the year Vietnam is swept by monsoons—tropical winds that bring storms of heavy rains, creating great floods. This colorful folktale attempts to explain how these monsoons came to be.

Long ago a beautiful princess was kept from marrying because her father, the Emperor, thought no one was good enough for her. She was very sad. Finally one day, two rich and handsome men showed up. One was Spirit of the Sea; the other was Spirit of the Mountain. The Emperor thought both men seemed worthy. Which one should he choose?

"Bring your betrothal gifts to the palace as soon as you can," he told the two men. "Whoever arrives first will marry the princess."

Spirit of the Sea hurried off to his ocean and commanded his subjects to bring him pearls, seafood, and other treasures. Spirit of the Mountain sent his subjects to bring mountain jewels and fruits. But because he cast a spell from a magic book, his gifts were collected in no time. That is how the Spirit of the Mountain arrived first at the palace. The Emperor was greatly pleased and sent the princess off with her husband-to-be.

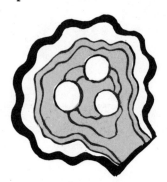

As Spirit of the Sea was on his way to the palace with his gifts, he saw the princess leaving with his rival. He was furious and commanded his army to steal the bride away. The wind began to blow, rain fell, and the ocean rose up. Huge waves broke over the land, flooding the people. The sea's creatures turned into soldiers and rushed over the land trying to catch the princess and Spirit of the Mountain. The bride and groom climbed the mountain as fast as they could. Their army threw tree trunks and boulders down the mountain at the sea soldiers. The poor people of Vietnam had their crops and homes washed away in the fighting.

Finally, Spirit of the Mountain climbed high enough to reach his magic book. He cast a spell to make his mountain grow even higher. Spirit of the Sea could no longer reach the bride and groom. Defeated, he went back to his ocean kingdom. But every year he tries again to defeat Spirit of the Mountain and win the princess. He sends storms and floods to the foot of the mountain. And that is why the monsoon comes to Vietnam.

GIVE A WATER PUPPET SHOW

The Vietnamese have a kind of puppet theater unlike any other. It is peformed with marionettes, but instead of using a solid stage, these puppets perform on water! It is said that for nearly 1,000 years, troupes of water puppeteers have traveled across Vietnam, performing on its many lakes and rivers. To create their theater, they set up screens of braided reeds on the lake. These screens keep the audience from seeing the marionettes being manipulated by the puppeteers (who may be standing in water up to their waists). The wooden puppets are painted brightly with red and gold. They stand from one and a half to two feet high and are attached to small wooden platforms. Each puppet is moved on the surface of the lake with underwater rods that can be thirty feet long. Wires, strings, and other gadgets are used to make the marionettes come alive. The chief character, the narrator, is known as Teu. He is a smiling marionette, and wears a red loincloth.

The very complicated methods of working these water marionettes are treasured secrets, but you may want to create your own version of the Vietnamese water puppet theater.

THE PUPPET STAGE

To create the effect of puppetry on water, cover a long rectangular table with an ocean-blue, floor-length cloth (you could use a sheet or a tablecloth). Or cover the table with paper (again it should reach the floor) and paint it with blue waves and ripples. This will be your Vietnamese lake.

The "lake" should be backed up to a wall, with just enough room between the wall and the table for the puppeteers, who will sit on the floor behind the table to move their characters. Read the play that follows and draw the three different scenes—the carambola tree, the hut, and the Mountain of Gold—on large pieces of paper. Tape each one on the wall as the scenes of the play change.

THE RODS

The Vietnamese water puppeteers use long rods to move their marionettes. You can create rods for your puppets by using flexible drinking straws. Each rod will be made of three straws. Pinch the end of one straw and feed it into the nonbending end of another. Now bend the flexible neck of the second straw to create a right angle. Pinch the end of the third straw and feed it into the newly bent end of the second straw. Bend the flexible neck of the third into a second right angle. Tape each connection to make it secure. You will need six rods for the six puppet characters.

THE PUPPETS

Trace the puppets on the following pages. Use your tracings as patterns to make your puppets on construction-weight paper. Color the puppets using a lot of red and gold trim. Tape your finished puppets to the short bent ends of the straw rods.

Now on with the show!

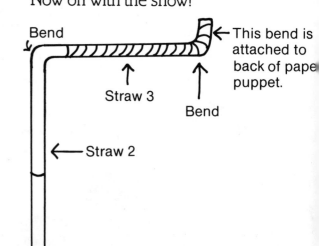

Bend

This bend is attached to back of paper puppet.

Straw 3

Bend

← Straw 2

Straw 1 →

Puppeteer holds rod here. →

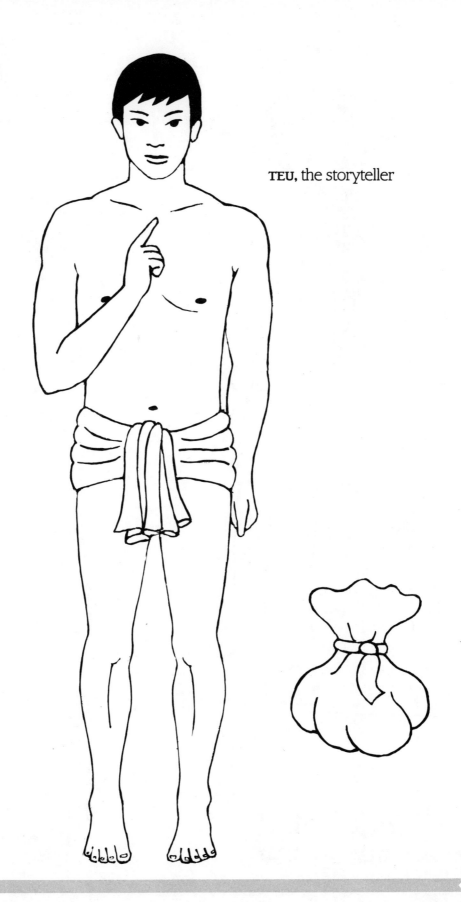

TEU, the storyteller

YOUNGER WIFE

ELDER WIFE

YOUNGER BROTHER

ELDER BROTHER

37

THE RAVEN, a magical bird

UNDER THE CARAMBOLA TREE

A VIETNAMESE FOLKTALE

CHARACTERS:
TEU, the storyteller
ELDER BROTHER, the greedy one
YOUNGER BROTHER, the generous one
THE RAVEN, a magical bird
ELDER WIFE, married to Elder Brother
YOUNGER WIFE, married to Younger Brother

SCENE I: **A field with a single, large fruit tree**

TEU: In a faraway village a wealthy farmer died, leaving his fortune to his two sons. Elder Brother was greedy and took all his father's riches for himself, giving Younger Brother only a single carambola tree. Every day Younger Brother watered and pruned his tree. But when the fruit finally ripened, a raven flew to the tree and began eating. **(He exits. Raven flies in and "sits" in the tree. Younger Brother enters.)**

YOUNGER BROTHER: Please, Raven, do not eat my fruit. If I do not have enough to sell at the market, my poor family will starve.

RAVEN: Don't worry about your family. I will pay for this fruit with gold. Go home now and bring back a bag that is 60 centimeters long to carry the gold in.

SCENE II: Inside Younger Brother's hut, which is furnished with a table and two simple chairs. Younger Wife is in room. Younger Brother enters.

YOUNGER WIFE: Hello, Husband, have you been to the market to sell our fruit?

YOUNGER BROTHER: Not yet. First I need a bag that is 60 centimeters long.

YOUNGER WIFE: What for?

YOUNGER BROTHER: I cannot yet say, but perhaps it will help us earn our fortune.

YOUNGER WIFE: All right. I will make the sack now. **(They exit.)**

SCENE III: The carambola tree once again. Raven is onstage. Younger Brother enters. A sack is taped to his hand.

YOUNGER BROTHER: Raven, I have brought the bag.

RAVEN: Climb aboard my back and we will fly across the sea to the Mountain of Gold. **(They fly back and forth across the stage a few times; then exit.)**

SCENE IV: **Younger Brother's hut. Younger Wife is onstage as Younger Brother enters carrying sack.**

YOUNGER BROTHER: Here! A gift for you! **(Younger Wife looks in sack.)**

YOUNGER WIFE: Why, this sack is filled with gold! We are rich!

YOUNGER BROTHER: Yes, it is true. I wish to celebrate my good fortune with Elder Brother, so I have invited him and his wife to visit us. **(A knocking sound is made offstage.)** That must be him now. Come in Elder Brother. **(Elder Brother and Elder Wife enter.)**

ELDER BROTHER: I have done you the favor of coming to your poor home. What do you want of me?

ELDER WIFE: My house is so much larger. It is so much finer. Perhaps I will send you my old table that I was going to throw away. It is still nicer than yours.

YOUNGER BROTHER: That will not be necessary. Look inside this bag.

ELDER WIFE: Gold! It is filled with gold!

ELDER BROTHER: Where did you get all this?

YOUNGER BROTHER: A raven has been eating the fruit of my carambola tree. When I complained, he told me to get a sack 60 centimeters long. Then he flew me on his back to the Mountain of Gold, where I filled up the sack.

ELDER BROTHER: I want that tree! I will trade you my fine house and all my riches for your tree and this little hut.

YOUNGER BROTHER: As you wish.

SCENE V: The carambola tree. Raven and Teu are onstage.

TEU: The next morning, Elder Brother hurried to the tree. There he found the raven eating its fruit. **(Teu exits.)**

ELDER BROTHER: Raven, you are eating my fruit. I will have nothing to sell at the market.

RAVEN: Do not worry, I will pay for the fruit with gold. Go home and get a sack that is 60 centimeters long. Then come back here.

SCENE VI: **The hut. Elder Wife is onstage as Elder Brother rushes in.**

ELDER BROTHER: Quick, wife! Sew me a sack that is 100 centimeters long.

ELDER WIFE: But Younger Brother's sack was only 60 centimeters long.

ELDER BROTHER: He was a fool. I will take a bigger bag so I can carry more money!

SCENE VII: **The sea. Mountain of Gold is in the background. Teu is onstage.**

TEU: The next morning, Elder Brother took a 100 centimeter bag to the tree. The raven invited him to climb upon his back. He flew Elder Brother across the sea to the Mountain of Gold where Elder Brother filled up his sack. Then Elder Brother climbed upon the raven's back for the flight home. **(Teu exits. Elder brother and the raven fly over the water.)**

RAVEN: You are so heavy, I am tired of carrying you. Younger Brother felt much lighter on my back.

ELDER BROTHER: Stupid bird, it is because you have been fooled. My bag is much larger and heavier than Younger Brother's.

RAVEN: It is you who has been stupid, for I cannot carry you any further. You will have your gold at the bottom of the sea. **(Raven drops Elder Brother off his back.)**

ELDER BROTHER: Aaaaaahhhhhh! **(Elder Brother and Raven exit stage. Teu enters.)**

TEU: Elder Brother never returned home. Younger Brother and his wife took pity upon Elder Wife and let her move in with them. They had enough gold so that they never again went to visit the raven in the carambola tree. Perhaps it is still there.

THE END

SAY IT IN VIETNAMESE

Vietnamese is a tonal language. That means the way you pronounce a word can change its meaning. Just the little word *ma* can be spoken in six different ways and have more than six different meanings! Little marks called diacritical marks, which appear over or under the letters, show how a word should be pronounced.

Here are a few Vietnamese words and phrases for you to try:

English	Vietnamese	How to Pronounce it
Hello	Ổng mạnh giỏi khổng	Ong mang zoi khong
I like you	Tỗi qủi ổng lẳm	Toi kwe ong lam
Thank you	Cảm ởn nhiều	Cam on new
Good-bye	Hẹn gắp lại	Hen gap lay

INDEX

ABOUT THE AUTHOR

Phyllis Shalant has written fiction and nonfiction for children, as well as magazine and newspaper articles and advertising. She also teaches creative writing to young people in Westchester, New York where she lives with her husband, two daughters and two cats.

WITHDRAWN